For Jess. **KS**
For Katrina Anne. **OS**

Thank you to Jean Rice from the Taronga Conservation Society Australia for help with Taronga's history and showing us behind the scenes at the zoo's archives. Thank you also to Anna McFarlane for introducing me to Jessie's story in the first place.—Kate

Thank you to Jean Rice, Neil and Sarah Boyd-Clark, Geoff Marsh at Susannah Place, the librarians and archivists at State Library of NSW, Vaughan Evans Library at the Australian National Maritime Museum, NSW State Archives, Museums of History NSW, Stanton Library and the remarkable time machine that is City of Sydney Archives.—Owen

First published by Allen & Unwin in 2024

Allen & Unwin
Cammeraygal Country
83 Alexander Street
Crows Nest NSW 2065
Australia
Phone: (61 2) 8425 0100
Email: info@allenandunwin.com
Web: www.allenandunwin.com

Allen & Unwin acknowledges the Traditional Owners of the Country on which we live and work.
We pay our respects to all Aboriginal and Torres Strait Islander Elders, past and present.

A catalogue record for this book is available from the National Library of Australia

ISBN 978 1 76118 030 9

We first learnt about this amazing true story from a wonderful exhibition of the same name at the Museum of Sydney and would like to thank the museum for the inspiration, as well as Jean Rice, Project Manager, Heritage, Capital Programs, Taronga Conservation Society Australia and the docuseries Tiny Oz (Northern Pictures).

For teaching resources, explore allenandunwin.com/learn

Illustration technique: pencil on paper, coloured in Photoshop

Cover and text design by Sandra Nobes
Set in 20 pt Baskerville
This book was printed in September 2024 by Hang Tai Printing Company Limited, China

3 5 7 9 10 8 6 4 2

How to Move a
ZOO

Kate Simpson
illustrated by Owen Swan

ALLEN&UNWIN
SYDNEY · MELBOURNE · AUCKLAND · LONDON

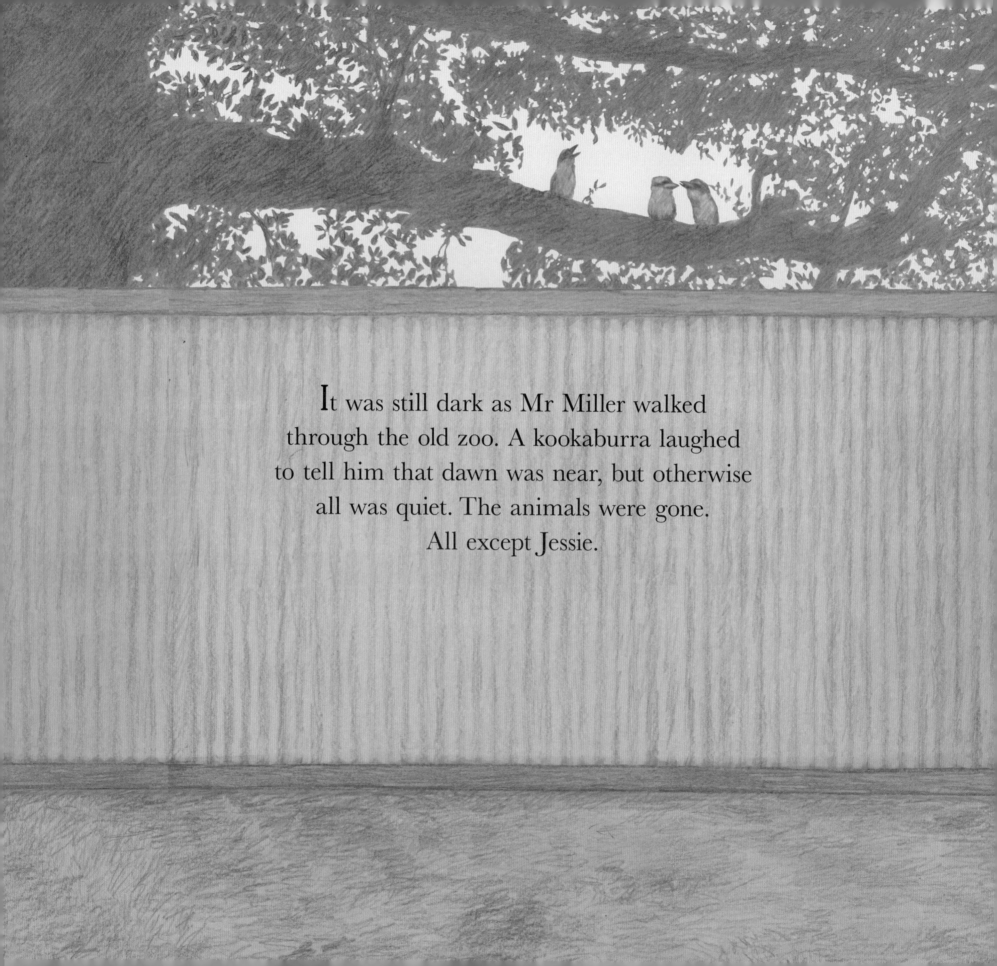

It was still dark as Mr Miller walked
through the old zoo. A kookaburra laughed
to tell him that dawn was near, but otherwise
all was quiet. The animals were gone.
All except Jessie.

For months, a slow parade of trucks
had headed north. On board, there were
crates and cages of every shape and size.

But no truck was coming for Jessie …
She would have to walk.

If the neighbours had known there was an elephant on their street, there'd have been children hanging out of every window.

But Jessie was silent on her soft feet. She didn't wake them.

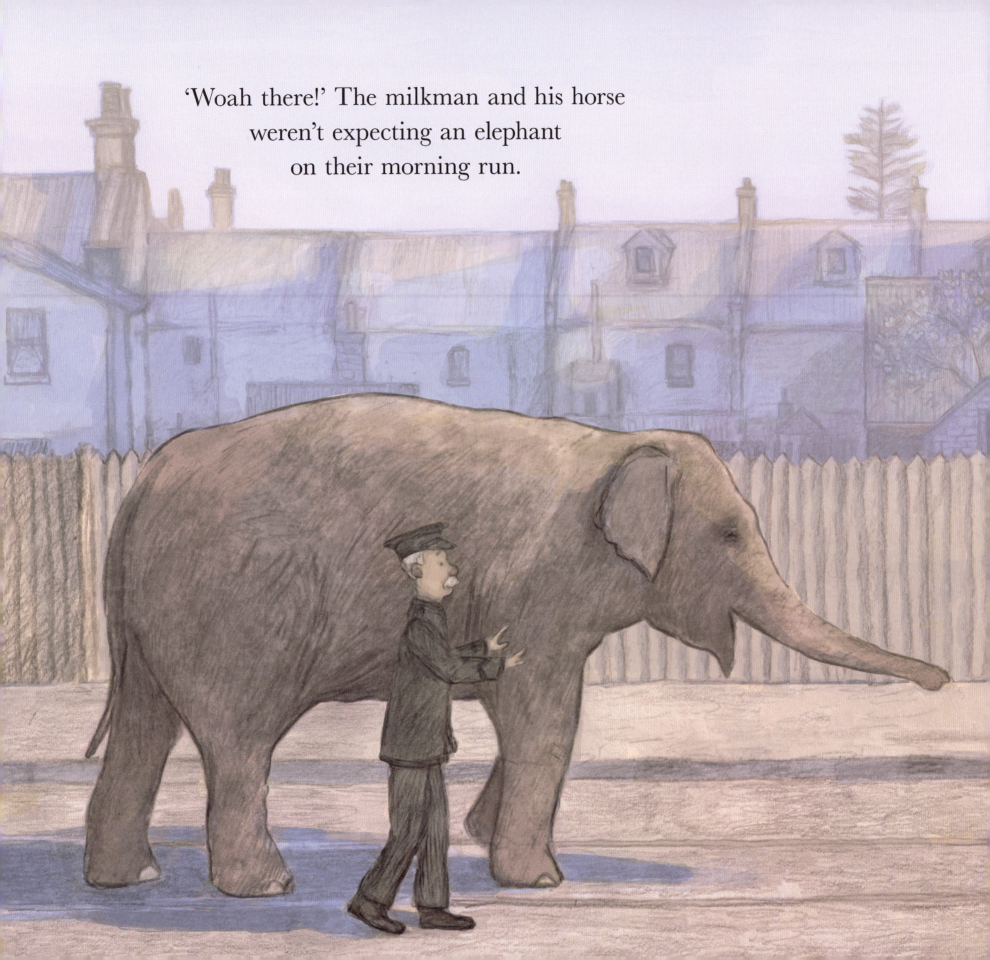

'Woah there!' The milkman and his horse
weren't expecting an elephant
on their morning run.

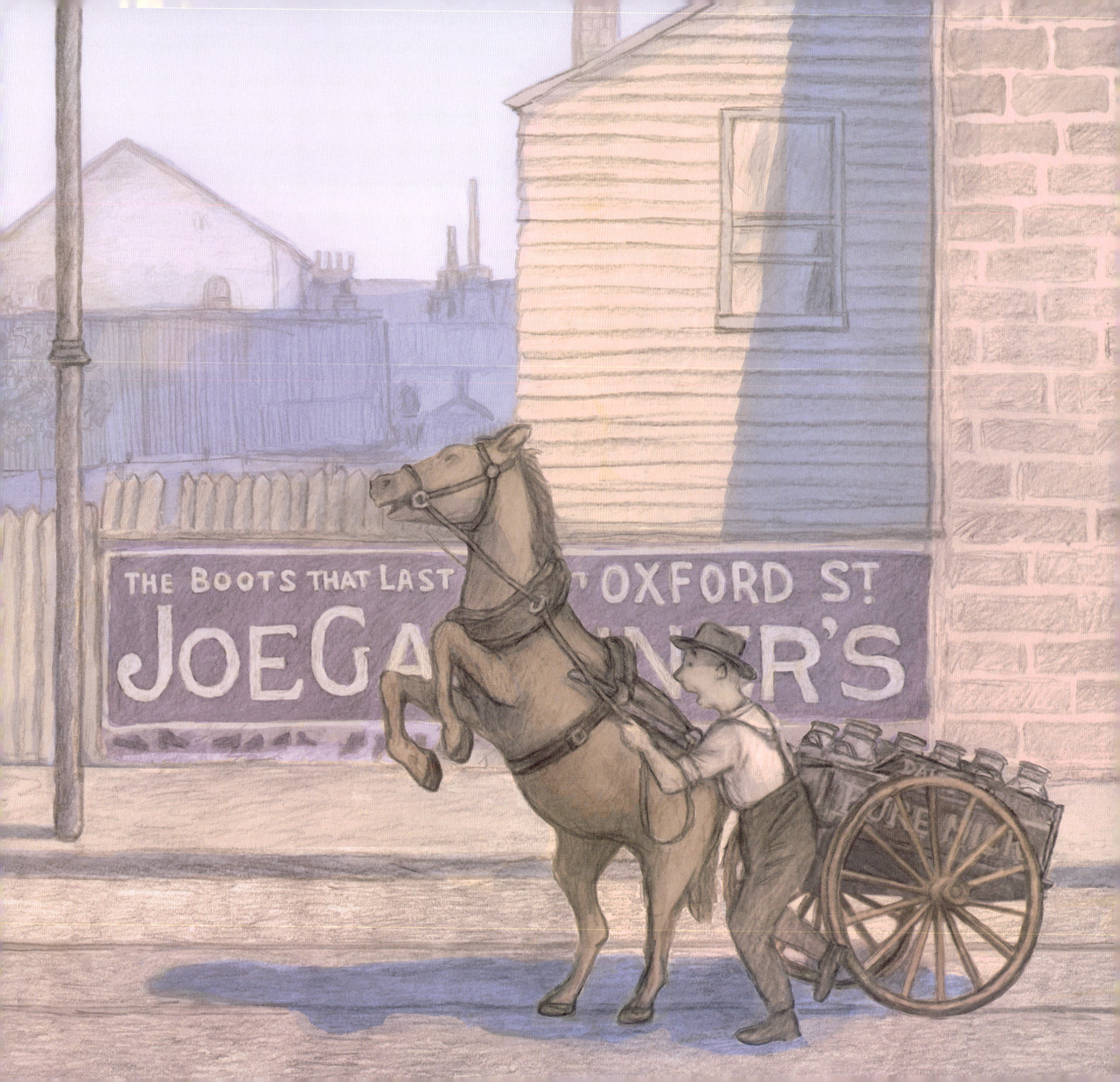
THE BOOTS THAT LAST
OXFORD ST

Mr Miller looked at Jessie. If she ran,
the damage would be worse than spilt milk.
But Jessie just flicked her trunk
and walked on.

In Taylor Square, an early riser looked out her window.
She blinked twice to be sure of what she was seeing.
'It's a bloomin' elephant!' she shouted to no one
in particular. Below, Jessie was unconcerned.
She knew she was an elephant.

Soon, there was a break in the buildings.
Trees. Grass beneath their feet.
Jessie trumpeted her pleasure.
'We're not there yet, girl.'

A ferry was waiting for them at Fort Macquarie.
Jessie looked at it, then reached for Mr Miller with her trunk.
She trusted him, but she wasn't so sure about boats.
'Come on now.' Mr Miller gave her a comforting pat.
'You'll be safe as houses.'

Jessie stood as still as a statue
across the harbour.

On the north side, the ferryman tied off with
a flourish. Jessie stepped out onto the pontoon.
'Easy there!'
'Watch it!'
The pontoon dipped under
Jessie's weight.

Step by step,
Jessie tiptoed across.

Mr Miller held his breath.

Jessie planted her feet firmly on the
solid ground of Bradleys Head.

At the zoo, a kookaburra laughed to announce Jessie's arrival.
Lions roared. Monkeys jabbered.
The elephant house shone in the sun.

Mr Miller slipped Jessie a bun from his pocket
and allowed himself a small smile.
Later, these paths would be full of children,
but for now it was just him and Jessie.
'Well, my girl,' he said, 'welcome home.'

Author's Note

Jessie the elephant was about eight years old when she arrived in Sydney in 1883 to be part of a new zoo being built at Moore Park. For a penny a turn, visitors could ride in a special saddle called a *howdah* on Jessie's back as she walked in a slow circuit within the zoo grounds.

The zoo at Moore Park was extremely popular, but before long, the zoological society had plans for something better: a large, modern zoo more suited to a growing city like Sydney.
But how does someone move a zoo?

In 1916, the Sydney Harbour Bridge had not yet been built. To cross the harbour by road was a long journey across five separate bridges. Instead, the zoo animals did what most people did at that time: they caught the ferry. Although the more dangerous animals were carefully contained, some, like Jessie, were trusted to take part of the journey on foot. One animal – a tiny sugar glider – travelled in a zookeeper's pocket. (If you look really closely at the illustrations, you might be able to find it.)

Today, Taronga Zoo is one of Sydney's most popular attractions. Elephant rides are a thing of the past; now the zoo has an elephant breeding program and raises money for elephant conservation. Animals are still moved to other zoos at times – some on the backs of trucks, others by aeroplane. But a journey like Jessie's – a quiet Sunday walk through Sydney's streets – is unlikely to ever happen again.

Jessie the elephant en route to
Taronga Zoological Park.
Courtesy of Dixson Library, State Library of
New South Wales – DL PX 165

Visitors at the entrance gates to
Taronga Zoological Park at the zoo's official opening.
Courtesy of Museums of History New South Wales –
StAC: NRS-4481-3-[7/16382B]-St5934